The
Lover
&
The
Revolutionary

T'challa Williams

"If art is to nourish the roots of our culture, society must set the artist free to follow his vision wherever it takes him."

John F. Kennedy

the lover

Kissing
Yes
Exposure
Sexy Thang
Mature
An Uncle's Cry
Rulership
No Matter
Saturate You
Go Head
Just Once
Brown Skin
Make Me
Cheba Cheba
Teenager
Cry
Truest
I don't like it
A lil ache
Inside
Beautiful days
Hey now
Thoughts of You
Musing
You
More
Watch Out now
Beautiful man
Right Now

&

the revolutionary

Speak to Me
In Speaking
Just Mad, no reason
Whatchu know
What Channel?
Melanistic Variant
Release Yourself
Motherless Child
Education
Wrong Wish
Felony
Litmus Paper
Karma
Growth
the return
Time
Word Play
Don't Shoot
Work
She Power
Lessons
Fight
Jimi
Blues
Answer the Call
Plateau
Just Grow
Free
Resolution
Assata

Acknowledgements

I write
I write when I'm up, down or indifferent
blank pages be my therapy and my blueprint
been writing for years, through fears and tears
this life is a journey
in both lanes
I remain
I am lover and I am revolutionary

Thank you for taking the time to share in this moment. Thank you to all of the men and women that have contributed to this path. I thank my lovers, my friends, my family and my fellow revolutionaries. Press on my people and change the world!

Your Sister in Arms,
T'challa

Hey fresh air,
May I breathe you,
Feel your gentle breeze kiss my cheek
Make troubles obsolete
Fill my insides with you till I renew
Fresh air, may I talk with you?

the lover

Kissing

I kissed a boy and felt the wind blow
Heard God's breath dance past my eardrum
Heard leaves float from beginning to end
Wind blew as the earth changed hues
And time subdued change
Bringing present into past range
Upon releasing from your embrace
I looked at your face
And felt chaste
Experience led me to understand
I kissed a man

Yes

Hot damn – hypnotic relaxation
Erotic connotations
Soul searching revelations
Yes and yes
Always and forever
No guess
Yours for the taking
No mess
Longing to awake
No stress
Loved eternally
Surely you jest
No baby
No games
Said it straight and made it plain
I was meant for you
And you were meant for me
But that which was meant, is so hard to be
I pledge my love to thee
Loved eternally
So shall it be
Let it be
Me

Exposure

Life is hard
Who said love would be different
I cannot shy away from a situation
Due to its degree of difficulty
I cannot deny you
And you cannot deny me
The mere idea of you makes me want to shout
Kindred spirits seeking each other out
Just to find what you were looking for
Just to arrive at an open door
Just to know you are loved more
Than what you initially believed
Something greater than you could conceive
You spark creativity in me
You bring words to the melodies playing in my heart
You make my soul bravado
And my loins staccato
Like the climax in an Italian opera show
With no intermission – without requesting permission
I want to expose true passion
Right on center stage
Unleash this juicy beast from her cage
Strip down this flesh to show you my bare core
Flawed and flawless
Libidos on pins and needles
Orgasms so close
A soft breath from your chest
Could make me explode
I want you
I want to breathe you deep
And smile as I watch you sleep
And reassure you each day
That passion this strong
Never goes away

Sexy Thang

I didn't want anyone to see me
And think entry
That's not allowed
Since I vowed
Crossed legs never beg
But often propositioned
On positions both sultry and compromising
My momma taught me the strength of a lady
And my grandma taught me less is more
Sexy is not the equivalent of a whore
True enticement engages a man's admiration
It creates ideas and fantasies
induces imagination
He can't imagine what your ass would look like
If it's spilling out of your pants at first glance
He can't think about breakfast in bed
When you have on more make-up than hair or vice versa
Ladies, let us move in moderation
take into consideration
Elimination of the excessive
In exchange for the suggestive
Embrace your natural beauty
And naturally
A man will embrace you

Mature

I have evolved
Desire revolved into
Something strongly centered on you
Loyal and true
Diligently pursued

You are

As precious as falling stars
That descend the way my heart does

when I see you

More valued than expensive cars
My house of love
Appreciating over the years
How much gratitude I have for you
Admiration, adulation
Elated at your trust
Excited I still make you lust
I want to unlock my soul to you
Expose your heart to my design
It may not make sense but
it is your scent I miss
The soft kiss from heart shaped lips
Strong hands holding my hips
Always equip
forever fantasizing about pleasing you
Teasing you
faithfully appeasing you

An Uncle's Cry
(*for John*)

My King
You must understand that your sovereignty demands
no explanation for or to no man
It is your right
and your plight
Those within your kingdom will follow suit with what you believe
do not be deceived
the truth needs no defense
and love is the recompense
people respect what you respect
but like dogs, your fear makes them second guess
if you are doing what you love
then relentlessly pursue
and those you wish to please will follow you
Royalty is claimed and not bequeathed
Love is what you feel
your own belief
Life teaches us that we can not change others
but we can change ourselves
and our light shines brightly enough to motivate the movement of
the people
From the street corner to the steeple
Don't be mad, be you
Rock on my brother and do what YOU do!
But know that we all have demons that feast on our insecurities
and truth be told only you can set you free
not location or vocation or provocation
just dedication to what you know to be true
Love who you will
We are all free to choose

Rulership

We look up
See the same moon
Spirits in tune
Moon beams cutting through clouds
The way your voice cuts through
To my core
Touching me
Caressing my heart
Breathing in synch
Comforted by silence
Nurtured by your laughter
Talking about the plight of a people
deterioration of hip hop
Can't stop won't stop
Pledging my allegiance
to a man
Who wants to know my dark side
Feel me ride
Walk in stride
Taste my essence
I can feel your love
Coursing through my veins
Embedded by sound
Moving round like
a kid ticking in a b-boy battle
Unravel this passion
Love on lock
Holding back
Just so I can unleash
Show you how you breached
The walls of my soul
Talking 'bout growing old
I'm loving the growing part
A connection like art
Played out like a Miles Davis song
Pushing my keys

Till I release
All my fantasies starring you
My fix it man
Doing all he can
But I'm just happy to hold your hand
Stand beside you
Encouraging my King
Take the kingdom baby
The world is yours
Your Queen swings swords
Cuts enemies and shouts
Fuck the system!!
Take possession of the land
And after your exploits
Come home lover man
And rain over me

No Matter

No matter
Without all the chatter
This love stands the test of time
You are the reason for my rhyme
The wind to my chime
Making my body sing
Your mere presence takes me back
To the emotions that made
Falling in love so memorable
That love that made you fascinated
with each part of your lover's body
Noticing how certain things make you feel
Touching me so deep I know that it is real
So real it scares me
The truth can't be denied
From the last to the first ride
You are my ideal mate
Holding the DNA to
A residual heartbeat
one that goes on for eternity
A love so strong it will
Transcend through lifetimes
It will be the basis of my daughter's fairy tales
the metal of my sons armor
transforming them into knights
Your love was always right
The fiber of what right is
I will drink of you always
Refilling you on all days
I know how to replenish your thirst
You know how to make me burst
You never make me curse
unless
accentuating great pleasure
One who's love I cannot measure
But you constantly display markers
so I know just how great your love is

Breath taking like standing atop Kilimanjaro;
overlooking the Motherland
Breath taking like sitting at the grand canyon
holding hands
But missing the sights because
Our hearts are overwhelmed with the fact that
we are together
always longing to be in reality
What we are in our hearts . . .
together

Saturate You

Drown you in my passion
This love has no rations
Unconditional and at attention
Awaiting the moment
to
Do what you mention
Limitless boundaries
Lullaby you to the sound of me
Our scent is your aroma therapy
Soothing away your tension
Relaxing your inhibitions
Energizing your inner vision
Renewing your strength
Magnifying your depth
increasing your length
I am your emulsifier
Taking you to higher levels
Of consciousness
Your Empress
Unlocking crown jewels
And exposing tools to your majesty
It would be a travesty not to partake
Or entertain the idea of ravishing me
These offerings are homage to you
Salute you when you hear it
No one's bolder than my soldier
Answering his call to duty
Your loyalty behooves me
Subdues me
Shower spoken apologies and pillow talk that woos me
Memories that bring a smile across my face
longing for your embrace
wishing no more to chase
that which is mine
awaiting your surrender to me
occurring all in due time

Go Head

Who am I to judge what makes you happy?
Manifest your own vision
Bring forth that which you trust
Love whom you must
Grope who you lust
From hair follicle to bust
To toenail polish
Publicly admonish not abolish
That is what your soul desires
Feed it
Cause you need it
Be free enough to see it long term
One that makes your passion yearn
And cry out in vulnerable moments
Where climax will not allow silence

Just Once

I am smitten
Seeking to overdose on your presence
Wanting to sit and stare at you
Until the heat of my gaze catches your attention
Put it on me
That doesn't happen!
Like the man said, I steal, I don't get stole on
Yet here I am
Looking and checking and waiting and
Wanting to ask questions
Wanting to know more about you
Wanting to hear your voice
Listen to you talk
Watch a smile light up your face
Wanting to play in your beard
as I lay across your chest
and listen to Marvin Gaye

Brown Skin

Brown skin lady
Quietly contemplating
Peacefully motivating
Moving and creating
Brown skinned lady
Skills that exceed understanding
Desires that maneuver like a hurricane wind
Whoom! . . .there you go again!
Always blazing your way
Got the whole world on the words that you say
Speak, thought, then teach
The love that makes you glow never out of reach
Family branches stretch across the land
Just to lend a hand
Love shown through gestures
Hearts that understand
Brown
Skin
Lady
Cocoa sheet protecting your femininity
Will that power rest in me
Will I glide when I walk
Provoke thought when I talk
Make somber melancholy into
Joy unspeakable joy
Brown skin
Brown skin
Her soul brightly shining from within
Lighting up any room she resides in
Wisdom and spirituality send cosmic invitations to knowledge
Experience has taught her more than any college
Her love has endured storms that the weather man has yet to
discover
Secured and held in place by the fact – she is a mother
Unconditional, profound and committed
Her presence commands as she stands
And she can't be out witted

Powerful, elegant
Poised, humble
Beautiful, brown skin
I love you

Make Me

You make me exhale slow
Stomach quiver from nerves
Stare off into the distance reminiscing
You make me
Long to hold you in the warmth of my mouth
For song, after song, after song, after
You make me want to stare into your eyes
Legs resting on your shoulders
You make me want to feel your face next to mine
As you lay me down
You make me wanna
Make me wanna
Sleep and wake to slow penetration
You keep she soaked with anticipation
Until next time
You make me wanna

Cheba Cheba

sometimes that green got me
desire shot me
all in my veins
wanting in vain
to satisfy my tense emotions
no sexual explosions
but intoxicating erosions
are my pacifier
taking me higher
but I'm floating like a feather on wind
destined to touch ground again
even though when I am floating
and gloating, I am hoping
a tree will catch me and plant me
into
different conditions
but my submission is nothing divine
to myself, i am just lying
biding my time
wishing versus qualitative deduction
plentiful productions of nothings
insanely watching seeds in packets in farmer's jackets
wondering why they wont grow
standing outside at midnight
wondering why the sun won't glow
bleak optimism
oxymoronically toting on izms
manifesting my souls schism
slaying my wisdom in clouded dismay
what more can I say?

Teenager

You are innocent I see it all over you
And he do too
Gold teeth like fangs
Waiting to suck life right out of you
What are you lured by
Nothing attractive or intelligent
I hear him talk
And sweet nothings
Are bitter bull crap
But you know that
And yet you let him lace
Fugazi thuggery
Like it was maple syrup sweet
Knowing your pancakes are the treat
And his plate is dirty
Are you taking blind eye
Why not some blind truth
Why not the faith of Ruth
Why not recognize you are Boaz worthy
Walk in your authority
Instead of feasting on crumbs
Communing with bums
I see your innocence
Like I am looking in the mirror
Never choose inferior
When you are superior
Selection is privileged
And the privileged are few
Don't let unworthy men
Break bread with you

Cry

What brings you
Moist
Wrinkled
Side eye of disdain
Shroud of pain
What swells you
Salty after taste
Unsolicited stomach crunch
No lunch
Deep breaths without meditation
Deflated
Sedated passions
Why knock
When
You
So easily invade
Taking over, cover
Contain, contaminated
Hated
And yet
When you leave
The waste is washed
The soul is emptied
Liberated from fears
Through
tears

Truest

Words drip like semen
And send me into gestation
Elation
Birth of love ensues
Passion subdues
I can't grab pen quick enough
Love flows from me
Love songs arouse me
Left to long like teenage love
Dark room
Late night conversations
Slipping through windows
Tipping through locked frames
Every time love calls
A touch
Last glance back
The slightest outstretched hand
Fingers that dare not release
Until
The Last Second Connection
Crossing yellow solid lines
Leaving me in a state of constant birth
Like a sleeping giant is awakened
I can't fake it
I cannot pretend
Cannot act like you don't bring
The best
Out of me
How could I ever separate
How could I not desire
My muse
You, my heart's haiku
My soul forever buried
With love that is true

I don't Like It

I don't like it
I thought about it
I gave the nonchalant laugh & changed my thoughts path
Just to come back to the same fork in the road
Not knowing has me on implode
Guess I don't like secrets
Or regrets
Or soft threats
I just don't like it
If it was as innocent as you say
Then why are complexities in the way
Wanting to explain but not ready at the same time
But you ascertain that the worry isn't mine
And yet
I don't like it

My confidence is telling me to leave it be
If it's meant to be he will stay with me
But that is without option
If that option factor increases
And transportation is of ease
Will you do what you please
At the expense of me
See
I don't like it

So now I am thinking about my own behavior
You could rate it or let me tell you later
Nonetheless
A harmless flirt will not catch me lying in dirt
But your words are dusty
Causing anxiety instead of trusting
My stomach is turning as I pen this note
Swallowing over lump in throat
Quiet, and in review
Of this relationship I have with you

Wanting conversation but not feeling like
The honest conversation I need
You'll heed
Your emotion constraints impede
Now I am wondering if you care about what I am thinking
Trying to help you while I am sinking
Wanting to love you and love on you
And yet, once again,
This is not a love poem
It is a cry from my heart
Transformed into art
Waiting for a patron's
appreciation

A lil ache

Missing you
Not that the distance is disconcerting
But I'm finding more moments
I want to share
I need to share
I crave you
I get busy and do other things but
That need to be connected to you
Becomes stronger
Substitutes are becoming less valued
I want the real thing
Your skin
Your dreamy eyes
Eyes on me
Seeing our future
Undressing and dressing me
All at the same time
Hands that touch every chance they get
Lips that speak without words
Thinking about spending every night
With you
I have to
My heart won't let me consider other options
She wants to be by your side
And so do I
But for now....
I am missing you

Inside

I feel like my whole world is getting ready to come undone
And it's not going to be any fun
And I shall be caught in the middle
Expected to decipher the oracle's riddle
But the riddle is not of words, it's numbers
And numbers are infinite
All I can say is , shit
I'm caught, all up in it
Once again I lay on the altar
Chest open
Exposed
Thinking about how he arose
And I lay, half dead
Half awake,
and wishing the other half would get the idea
but it never does
and then here I am again
naked
chest open
acid rain drenching my soul
leaving holes the size of grains of sand
but none touch
its just a bunch of emptiness
I can't confess
I'm just undressed
Chest open
No sound
Just salt water running from my planet to the universe
But nothing is universal
It all feels like a curse
Life is cursed – death blessed
How do I escape this mess
I wish I could fly
Because I would be fruitful and multiply a whole other planet
And leave this bullshit behind me
Because right now
My chest is open

The vultures are having sautéed heartache with fillet of soul
I need to be closed to be whole

Apotheosis

I use to love the ladies
Yeah, they did something for my flesh
That I'll try to explain
Sweet aroma invading my brain
Making me wonder if
You taste as good as you smell
Soft shoulders
Shaved legs
Full lips and round hips
Hidden under impressive ensembles
 I love how well you pick up on my word play
And that look you give
That says
Don't play! You'll mess around and
Start what you can't finish
Egos diminished
By domineering prowess
Until you are up against another female
Who knows the games we play, so well
The thought of getting a smile from you
Makes my lips swell
I mean
I use to love the ladies
We are so beautiful
And extremely sexy
Who better to appreciate every curve of your body
And verse of your speech
Than me?
Men forget
They forget to listen
Forget about the nape of your neck
And elbows and
The intimacy that comes before penetration
No, I am not a man
I don't need toys and gadgets
To appreciate all that you are
All I need are my ears and imagination

They will help me explore every part of you
Soft kisses to your spine
Full lips along your collar bone
Gazes of awe over your beauty
No hurried breathing or sprints to insert
Just soft French kisses
That make the hairs on your body alert
Yeah, I use to love the ladies
Now I window shop
Admire your sensuality from a distance
Loving your confidence and resilience
Boldly move forward my dear
Strut your stuff with no fear
And I will simply look on
From over here

Beautiful days

Beautiful days are coming
Days where I don my sundress
Place helmet
And
Jump on backside
Riding with my lover
Taking in the beauty of this earth

The aroma of our love
Seeping from our clothes and
into the atmosphere
Our pollen
Potent enough to bring life back to bees
Grow trees
Produce more seeds
Replenish this earth
Off of the scent of us
Imagine what saturated sheets could produce
Once fluids removed and bottled up
Together we are the source
Pure energy
Capable of anything

Hey Now

I might be holding my breath
Waiting to hear from you
Reading messages
Hearing songs
Looking at pictures
My senses are filled with you
Would rather body cavity
Play blanket to your member
Rather ride you till you drool
Because your mouth has been open from awe
So long
Rather plant kisses from below your navel
To your glistening crown
Rather sit behind you and run my hands across your frame
Release your tensions
Press knots out with my hands
And
hold you
Just hold you
Close to my bosom
So my heartbeat be lullaby
My love be peace
And my slightest touch transports you to heavenly places

Thoughts of you

Wee hours found me
Thinking of you
Arms wrapped around your neck and
Kissing you slow
Fingers caressing nape
Lips touching gently
Pressure applied at sloth pace
Revealing palpability
Then
Small space made way for our tongues
Making out like teenagers
Inhaling each other; who needs air
Daring curfews
Captured by passion
Locked in each other's humidity
While heat makes clothes unbearable
This that we share is comparable
To film and fantasy
Though you and me be
Average joe and jane
Love cascading off mountain plains
Falling into slopes of hopelessness
Lying in valleys exposed
Unclothed and basking in the light of love

Musing

Can you feel my thoughts?
Is my voice a soft whisper
A hand gently caressing forearm
My emotions, are they strong enough to pull you in?
My mind falls on you
As if an energy source has locked me in
I don't mind this path because it leads to familiar
I just don't want to be caught up in rapture of you
Only to find
Me
In the room
alone
I know this isn't the case
I'm enjoying the journey
Yet this burning
Insusceptible to reproach
Coaxed ambition to attain
that from which others refrain
I'm not built that way
Mean what I say
And pursue hearts desire
Though love trumps goals
I'm bold
And will not fold
Heart be that important
Love will not be denied
Even if hearts be sacrificed

You

My quiet moments are filled with
Reflections of you
Meditation of touch
I wonder if I am thinking too much
But there is peace
In thoughts of you

More....

You have more control
More control over me than any other
I sense your energy
Moving me
Stirring me up
Pulling me into you
I like you having control
Like a child craves structured atmosphere
I need you
I believe your touch will continue to unravel me
Yet I am excited about coming undone
Disassemble my moving parts
Throw out the trash
Refurbish me lover
Rebuild me
So that this heart continues to beat
Only for you

Watch Out Now!

Hey!
Don't you be eye ballin' me
I'm older than you think
And before you could even blink
I'll have you feeling like a school boy with a crush
Make the dark chocolate brothas blush
Plush, supple & juicy
Engaging smile and feminine wiles
Accessorize my sexual energy
Drawing you into me
Dominant yet submissive
Strong enough to take all you have to give and then some
Smiling at the well-endowed like yum-yum!
I'll do what the young girls can't
& what them bougie chicks ain't
Love so insatiable
It makes the strongest brothas faint
Hood with class
Class with sass
Intelligent with wit sharp as glass
I'm blended better than a strong mixed drink
Just when you think you can handle it
Sexy brown will have you at your brink
Trying to get your high down
Tastes so good you'll crave me when you dream
Wake up laying in your own cream
Freaky enough to lick you clean!
I'm mean & keen
Make love burst like the sun bringing forth the dawn
Giving you thirsty brothas that for which you long
You won't be able to be proud
I'll make you say it loud
Got more tricks than a little bit
This is who's what?
This is my . . .
Damn!
Just don't be eye ballin' me

As you can see
I'm up for a challenge
You ready for defeat?

Beautiful Man

There are so many things I want
So many things I need
And a beautiful black man is a necessity indeed
Now, don't get me wrong
God has created some hella-fine men
From Hawaii to Australia and back again
But there isn't one that makes me pause
Like a bad ass black man
You know a man so refined that you have to
Stop what you are doing so you can get a good look
Ladies, you know what I'm talking about
That brother with the flawless haircut
Pretty white teeth, clean fingernails
Ironed clothes, and simple jewelry; nothing gaudy
A man doesn't need to show you all of that
Cologne smelling like Thanksgiving dinner
And your stomach aches from hunger
Because you KNOW Thanksgiving only comes once a year
Shit, I'm hungry now
And I just can't see how
To live without you
Strong, charismatic and in control
Rational mindset piercing my soul
Making me get to the heart of matters
No frivolous chatter but
Thought provoking remnants of the future
Black man you heal my wounds like a suture
And I just can't see how to live without you
And who said you weren't a father
Mr. Little League-basketball coach slash
Karate instructor slash youth fellowship leader and mentor
Always lending a hand when necessary
Or voluntary
And it is you I wish to marry
And we don't need a prenup
As long as you call me butter cup
Cause I just can't see how

To live without you
You set precedence for many to come
Even though your history has come undone
I see truth in your eyes
Every night when we lie
And you say
All you need is to feel me close at night
And everything will be alright
And I just can't see how to live without you

Right Now

Perfect timing
No such thing
Love shows up abruptly
Demands your attention
Enthralls you in passion
And dares you to look away

The Revolutionary

What is the purpose of a dream
Is it to keep the brain active
If so, why can't we make it productive thought
Dream dreams of revelation, scientific connotations
Wise innovations
Thoughts provoking action, provoking change
Theories without range

Speak To Me

I am not at war with another country
I am at odds with lady liberty herself
Failing to experience her wealth
Surely is no fault of my own
Assistance to a dream
Should be available to her believers
But she seems to have stopped believing in me
Constantly regurgitating her ideals
But never removing her blindfold to see my obstacles
Too busy handing out Prozac scripts
And telling me what realities my imagination is drawing up
I am no Walt Disney
But there is a Walt Disney World
However, the world I seek
Keeps hiding from me
But my life is not a game
And I am not insane

In Speaking...

While speaking to black
I saw what he lacked
Damn my man what is that?
Gotta get my hustle on
Gotta floss my ice
Gotta keep it real
Gotta get my loot on & drop this album
"The Man", is holding me down
Shit is hard right now!
While speaking to black I heard his theory
On blackology, the new found wisdom of black
Fuck black
I'm African
Nigga fuck you,
You black, and you dumb
Name change does not reflect the content of your intellect
Redefining yourself goes deeper than the label
If you take the label off a can of soup
And replace it with the label for a can of beans,
You still have a can whose contents will remain unknown
Until it is opened
Just because you follow the masses
In their search for passes
Into the next level
Does not mean you are intelligent
A stray dog will follow you home if you feed it
Your gesture does not reflect
your desire to teach him how to survive
You just gave him a little something; enough to stay alive
In speaking to black I realized...

Just Mad, no reason

Sometimes I feel like people ain't shit
Loyal muthafuckas always quit
Kids don't turn out the way you dreamt
And most men you meet come unequipped
Bitches lie to you
And then with your man
And THAT hoe's out fucking every hole he can
It's a jacked up world we dwell in
I would say live
But when you really need shit
Nothing ever gives
And when you get tired of the full court press
Your family finds a way to get down with the mess
So you take to create
A balance in this terror dome
Then you realize
Hell has become your home
Mad and frustrated
With your heart full of treason
You looking at everybody like,
"PLEASE, give me a reason!"
Petty shit ticks you off
Nothing ever makes you soft
You wishing all the punk ass niggas
Would step the fuck off
Put the clip in the tool
And start actin a fool
No peace coming to you
Unless you use violence
I think I'll taste this barrel head
And have a moment of silence

Whatchu Know?

What do you know about a revolution?
About unavoidable evolution
Change is the equivalent of time
Revolution is change
Time has no end
So what do you know about it
Are you even conscious?
Do you believe you are not a chain in this link?
Got ya nose up like evolution stink
What do you think?
That blood and sweat have no odor
That tortured flesh heals back
To what it was before
You will never be who you were
And who you are presently
Is not the final composite of who you will be
Wake your ass up!
Recognize
All roads do not lead to freedom
But you have to walk it
In order to know where you are going
And yes,
Your eyes must be open
In order for you to move from where you stand
If you are even standing at all

What Channel?

Where is your mind
When you are watching television
Has it snuck off to complete some secret mission
What does it do
Is it gathering clues
Your body becomes stagnant
Transformed like voodoo
entranced by subliminal messages
overwhelmed by advertisement
buy this and buy that
for what
not because it is a necessity of life
deemed valuable to your existence on this planet
just buy it to put money in our pocket
always making money off someone else
does the world have a gambling problem
well CT lotto says, "you can't win if you don't play"
children chasing transmitted pipe dreams
my child metamorphosis into the goddess gimme
now she believes that all desires are handed over
and not worked for
all ideals and methods of survival
are misconstrued by the idiot box
constructive thinking is not necessary
because the remote control does it all
turn it on – turn it off – turn it on – turn it off
our mind needs some down time
from this moment we are suspended in time
however, time does not stop for us
you must be on time
keeping time
time for kids and time for man and time for woman
and time has not stopped
the seconds continue to be added up
and when I looked to check the clock
I realized five hours had gone by and
I haven't done anything at all

So I asked myself
Where were you when the TV was on?

Melanistic Variant

Can that be me?
A variation of pigmentation
Or a representation of the African Diaspora
Master saw the potential of our being
Feared what he was seeing
And in a synch
Obtained instructions from Willie Lynch
Amidst the exchange, our souls were rearranged
We ignored the hieroglyphic notes
Forgot the tenacity of the Massai
The determination of the Zulu
But the Caucasoid knew
He understands the power of a wronged people
Determined to rise up
Hell bent on revenge
The idea makes them cringe
Nauseous at the concept of repatriation or reparations
For an unacknowledged nation or nations
Africans are not alone in this struggle
US history makes it plain
Many colors ridiculed for others peoples gain
In a land built on the rape of culture
And conformity to greed
Taking more from the land than what we really need
Murdered
Watching the blood of Kings and Queens flow through city streets
We are a mighty people
We cannot succumb to defeat
Do not be insane
Our melanistic variant
Represents our kinship
To a strong and innovative history
We naturally circumvent bullshit
We cannot comprehend what it means to quit
Determination to survive
Helps me thrive
When you find that your spirit won't allow you to settle

And you just can't condone mediocrity and idiocy
Please know that THAT discomfort
Is the blood of your ancestors
Pumping to your spirit
Take heed - don't fear it
Your survival in this world
Is dependent on your ability to listen to your soul
Be bold
Your stories are laced in gold
Ageless
& waiting to be told

Release Yourself

This mundane day is daunting to me
Smothering my spirit in dark clouds
Suffocating my joy
I like to be happy and more so than that
I like to be busy
But that isn't happening
In my boredom I am evaluating all contributing aspects to my life
My strife
Being a wife
in an instant I could easily do away with all the drama
Even being a mama is getting on my nerves
Is that absurd?
Certain things just aren't enjoyable to me anymore
Not looking forward to what a day has in store
Because I know that bitch is a bore
And she keeps staring at me
Asking me to play with her
But she has no toys to share and no eyes to stare
How can I engage with someone who can't see me
Why can't you see me
I am looking at myself wondering
is there something I need to change about me
But I am the lock not the key
Where is my locksmith
I am rusting up and joints are stiff
Gotta exercise my gift but it is behind the door
Jumping up and down with no sound
Just screaming faces
Cold cases
Waiting to be picked up again
To blow in the wind and be appreciated like a cool summer breeze
Instead I am stuck on brain freeze
Waiting for someone with no knowledge of me
To pay me what I am worth
Bump waiting
I'll pay myself
Blow the hinges off the lock and set my spirit free

Tactics seem drastic but that is the price that must be paid
I cannot be a slave

Motherless Child

Sometimes
Sometimes I feel like a motherless child
left to run in the wild
Sentenced to dwell in houses
That will never be homes
Kitchens with filthy chrome
places where the food is gone
My hair is dirty and knotted up
those who pass by,
Pass by my cup
Saliva satisfies my thirst
A homeless child abandoned since birth
What did you have me for
Was I the keep-a-nigga-baby that didn't work
So you left me for some jerk
And now you sit in barren rooms
I wish you had a barren womb
Then I wouldn't have to endure this hell
Because your boosting ass went to jail
Do you think those clothes were for me?
No, nothing you do ever seems to be
Why did you do this to me
Why'd you leave me at three
No childhood games on your knee
No pity pat or Candyland
Because you were determined to love your man
And not your seed
Heart filled with greed
Now as my failing heart bleeds
I am faced with the reality of supplying my own needs
What do you think I will choose?
What options does a young girl have?
When there is no foundation for her to grab
Go with what comes easy
So next time when you see me
Remember
Twenty-dollar blow

Forty-dollar lay
I don't care what nobody has to say
You passed my cup when I openly asked
So now I gotta sell my ass

Education

What is an education?
Mental elation and soul gratification
A level of awareness to a legally blind nation
And what is the ramification of not having the benefit
What does the lack of such represent
The reflection of a race of people's discontent
Tell me what is actually meant
When the mind won't circumvent
And creation is replaced by duplication
Bites and bits
Glamour and glitz
Lies dressed up in camouflage
Vegetables dressed up like hogs
Everybody is your dog
Oh, I'm a pet now?
Often times I wonder
How do you define education in your mind
Is it acquired over time
And how much time is enough
And why do you learn all this stuff
Are you going through assimilation?
Or are you in the process of escaping
This matrix of a world
That keeps elating me
Degrading me, defacing me
Taking me through the motions
Of a very polluted ocean
Where knowledge of self has drowned
And love just can't be found
They took religion to the pound
As the spirit seeks higher ground
My soul is power bound
Because my mind deciphers sound

Wrong Wish

I wished for death today with no shame
Close to losing my mental reigns
There is no willingness to hear me
No desire to understand me
Just commands
      and demands
         and reprimands
             And angst against me
             If you hate me so
             Even in fleeting moments
             Don't vent
             Leave me the fuck alone
             Because the strain on my brain
             Is tapping on my sanity
             and self-esteem is vanity
             and ambition is selfishness
             and loving myself is neglect of you
             But if I am dead what will you do?
             Warning signs have gone unnoticed
And transformed into cleverly ignored artwork
             Well, this bitch (as you called me)
             Wants her life back
             This itch
             that I have
             will be scratched
             By me
             I know where it is and how to relieve it
But you have never taken the time to know who I am
             To understand what makes me
             You spend your time
             relishing
             in finding ways to break me
             Well
             I'm not glass – I don't break easily
             And my memories are elephants
             And my revenge is cold pizza
             And a slowly smoked cigarette

With no regrets
My anger can be satisfied
Quicker than yours
I simply choose not to allow evil through my doors
However
You *are* a tempting target
And this motherfuckin bitch
Wants your ass on the market
But I told her
Calm down
Evil is not her crown
But your words
Your multitude of words
Made me want to drown my kindness
In venom lakes
Slit your throat as you sleep
So there would be no peep
These angry feelings I dare not keep
Because thoughts can manifest
and
I like your blue shirt better than your black suit
From my anger you will recoup – this time
But next time
Don't fuck with me
Or my beast
Will be unleashed to feast
& Your peace
Will be still

Felony

Have you ever been convicted of a felony?
Have you ever been convicted of a felony?
Have you ever been convicted?
Convicted enough to slap your lady
Convicted enough to pull the trigger
Pull the trigger
Pull the trigger
I dare you nigga
Tempted and teased
Set up and eased
Into a system designed to break down your very existence
You wanna know why the niggas call us bitches
Because as they sit inside of the tiny little compartment
Eating their last pack of oodles and noodles
Sipping coffee
Wondering why his lady don't visit
Why ma don't accept his calls
Another may wonder why
The sister came to tell him about
the brotha she gave the ass to
damn
collected as society's rejected
neglected by midnight's silent whisper
just to kiss her is a mere memory
and memories of life as the free and un-oppressed
suppressed by that which others obsess
I guess
I am public enemy
Openly under attack
As all the support sits back
And views the massacre
On the idiot box
Channel – 6 Cops, Channel –11 Family Matters
Do we really care about when a cop does his job
That is to be expected
So who is the target audience for Cops and what is the message
To glamorize that which damages us is the utmost disrespect

So if you think you served 2 to 3
And now you are finished
Paid your debt to society,
Now you ain't in it, think again
My incarcerated friend
Your record is blemished
And life as you know it has been diminished

Litmus Paper

Taken and stored
Mine and yours
Untold and with no remorse
My guess is
This isn't just happening in Texas
Doctors have tipped off and done what they please
Said it in the name of science
With too much ease
Licensed to cure disease
But science is far from being
The arena it once was
A club of testers
Trying to debug the bug they placed
Lying to my face
And carting my DNA
To a secret database
You need my permission of course
Parents left with no recourse
Because you believe the paperwork to be
Too engaging, too time consuming
While with my baby's blood
You seem to be playing
A violation of the highest protocol
I could run up in a lab
And slap all of ya'll
Or better yet invite you to my coffee shop
Where dine-in utensils prick
Just a little bit
And take your litmus sample
To ample rooms of zoom and doom
But wait
Perhaps a simple handshake
A gesture of kindness
But deceptive to the meek
Removing the lie from the words that I speak
Allowing me to sneak
Precocious sweat glands – off into the distance

To uncharted lands
Would you let me
Would you buy it
If I said it was done
In the name
Of
Science?

Karma

Do those that need persecution get vindication
Do those who need vindication get persecuted
Definition uprooted
Is it about the person
Or the act
That makes this circle of life
Push what you send out
360 back
Do new acts stop it at the 90th degree
Did your good to someone else
Erase your wrong on me
Is my vengeance blind hope
Justice on dope
Merely the idea of something
Designed to help me cope

Growth

High of possibilities
Excited about the meanderings of theories
Are you listening to me, he or she
Me being societal ideologies
He is your conviction
She is wrapped in your skin
Each whispering sweet nothings
Debating and arguing of wanting
Execution is daunting
But don't be enraged
If you want to see progression
You must engage

the return

the junkies have returned
the junkies have returned
they have come back to remind us that
they never really left us in the first place
people's un-addressed needs and increasing greed's
have caused them to resurface
what's that you say
addicted to what
addicted to freaky sex in a Cineplex
addicted to the thong song
and how well my man does me wrong
and the view they queue up sally's crack everyday
when I get my video attack

addicted to what
addicted to Hennessey and coke
and them dutches that make me choke
after that philly I coped from Millie
dusted me silly
made me fuck Billy with the big Willie
and Millie too
shit
i won't remember
december

addicted to what
addicted to a little sniff unnoticed whiff
light that phat spliff
a little lick here
a little pill there
addicted to lacing it
smoking it chasing it
facing it never
wasting it always
wet days dry days cold days
hiiiiiiiiiii days
hi days

addicted to what
addicted to watching
peeping, seeking to discover
what you do with your day
as I waist mine
whose world, our world
the real world where
big brother watched survivors obey road rules for a real chance at the
flavor of bullshit
something as innocent as totally hidden video
totally exposing us to a need that
though unrecognized is constantly fed
why you wanna know what's inside my head
I'm just addicted

Time

A gift we constantly neglect
An undervalued asset
We see it as depreciating
When it's really appreciating and yet unappreciated
Unrelated, and unrelenting on its speed
Tick-tocking away and we never take heed
Until the pressure makes us shout
TIME IS RUNNING OUT!
What will you do
As this clock winds down for you
What will you render your thoughts to
Relinquish your actions to
Put your hands in momentum to
Push your motivation towards
Competition of no reward
Or at least intangible
A race you need to enter but your mind says you're ineligible
Do you follow your heart
Bless through your art
Or aimlessly stand around
Wondering where art thou
I sayest where art thou
Tho thou beest and doth not do

Lessons

We are disappointed
Devastated, when things
Do not turnout the way we want
You are not clairvoyant
Every choice we make has a lesson to be learned
And it is this lesson's turn
You can choose to learn
Or ignore, however
Ignorance delays the blessings that are in store
But it does not take away from the fact
There is something about this situation
That your understanding lacks
You need to pass this act
Or forever be stuck at intermission
Ignorance is synonymous with repetition

Good lessons hurt a little
& have a tendency to bend us in ways
we do not want to stretch to
we want to go around when the only way is through
so what
you don't like it
so what
your flesh is uncomfortable
it is not as uncomfortable as it could be
times like this
reflecting on my ancestors moves me
all the mistreatment they went through . . .
murdered without explanation
beat beyond recognition for
having a piano
or blinking at a white woman
or speaking properly when we are supposed to be
too ignorant to speak at all
all in an effort to make us fall
keep us small

I don't have any of these challenges right now
So what right do I have to complain about a little discomfort?
Shut up and learn the lesson
Is it easier to be bitter than to change?
The end of bitterness is un-colonized concepts
Surrounded by selfishness and bubbling pits of the seven deadly sins
Flames do not dance on my heart
My tears of joy prevent them from gaining momentum
If God wants us to change,
Then only the end result will develop us
Into wiser people of God.
Why is that so odd?
Why don't we want to be better?
Is it because success requires maintenance
& maintenance requires discipline
discipline requires obedience
& obedience is better than sacrifice
yet here we are with different parts speaking to us
at the same time
we need to evaluate what part of us we are looking to satisfy
flesh or spirit?
The word can help you hear it
But illiteracy is not an option
You can't always go in,
Guns blazing
Some fights require planning
Some planning requires patience
Patience requires faith, &
Faith without works is dead . . .

Word Play

Who will hold my truth
Unfurl imaginations
Refraction
Didactic
Disintegrate my soul
Kick the pieces around
Pick through my molecules
Spit pon di earth
Mold clay of me
Rooted in the propers
Extension of my fathers
Father, father
Who will expose raw flesh
And muscle tissue
MRI this shit
And fertilize dreams deferred
Subvert contaminates
Murder genetic modification of
Nurture my core
Stretch me till I scream stop
Then change direction
So I am not afraid of my reflection
Deflection
Multiplied by subsidiaries
Decipher intentions
No invention
No modification
De-vel-op-ment

Who will take unknown materials
Muse over
And engineer answers
Master architect
Creating archetype
I am not what you know
Gotta lose yourself
For vision to be 20/20

Stand immotile at 90
But meet at 360 without moving
Amalgamate synergies
Reform
Me

Don't Shoot

You keep telling us to trust you
Have faith in you
You will handle judiciously
Fuck that
Y'all some liars
Everyone else gets to exact their type of justice
On people of color
But we can't do the same
So what…you want my okay so you can murder me at will
What…you want me to stand still
So you can take me out?
Fuck You!
I'm not laying my life down for you!
If you want it
Come and get it
I got 400 years of repressed anger inside me
I know my history
I am a Warrior!
As a Queen I specialize in strategic warfare
I was BUILT to fight for and save my family
I'm not distracted by reality TV
And all that natural hair versus weave
Fat obese skinny is cuter
Light skin dark skin Willie Lynch SHIT!!!
I see you
Been watching all my life
As I approach my fortieth year
It needs to be one the Oppressor fears
I'm educated
Calculated
Committed
Focused
And mad as hell
No justice
No peace
No justice
No got damn peace

Work

Underpaid and under appreciated
Skills under arrest
Creatively oppressed
Management suppressing like they name is mucinex
And who's next?
Assassination of character
While integrity is lacking her full ability to flourish
My soul's not being nourished
But I'm not discouraged
I am a warrior of an elite tribe
And though you cannot sense my vibe
I still move forward in pride
Our paths don't coincide
I'm moving up while you moving along
Lyrics to two different songs
You humming melancholy
And I'm stomping out war songs
I Cheech & Chong
Meditate long
On the elaborate collaboration of wisdom and intellect
Thoughts dissect
No regret
I'm not bending to this level
I'm lacing my boots
Positioned for acceleration
Bottom level obliteration
Middle tier consideration
High achiever proliferation

She Power

I am an advocate of anything
that deals with the uplifting of She
and yes
this is inclusive of he
and me
but unhappy me
creates unstable we
no praise to thee
discontent breeds calamity
why should women work hard
and receive hardly
from powers that be
or he
the worlds needs me
She, that is
so why should compensation
or appreciation
not be the equivalent
of the air you breathe
quick to cleave and leave
at the same time
love She
and reap the benefit of reciprocation
neglect She
and witness the decimation of a nation

FIGHT

I just don't want to
Just don't want to
Be
Here
No excitement about the future
Of
Here
No joy in my veins fueled by possibilities
For in what has been made possible
I see no reassurance
Of a different tomorrow
The monotony of these 24 hours
Is predicated by unproductiveness of the last
Stuck repeating the past
Angered by the effervescence of the present
Bright shining light
Coupled with a dim imagination
Shadowed by circumstances and situations
Don't want to
No escape route
No rope thrown down from the mountain top by my rescuer
Because they have not reached the top yet
Together we fail
Fall
Call
Brawl
Fight against the winds
Just to be blown away by what others say
Measured against the immeasurable
Subtracting double negatives
And simplifying fractions
Cutting pie to the point where I have no slice
Rolling dice in a crap game
Finding all this mess lame
Different views of the same
Forcing this wild to tame
And killing me all at the same time

The more you see
The more I fight to be me
Life keeps ducking my overhand Wright
Gotta come with the left uppercut
But I must use my gut
And my gate has lost too much weight
But not enough to change divisions
So I keep throwing these blows till I have precision
Precision enough to knock this life out
And win this bout

Jimi

I feel like liberation is running through my veins
Each time he strums the guitar
It stops me
I count my breath
Bright colors kaleidoscope across the backdrop of my mind
Eyes closed
Heart full
And he plays
I feel
Alive
I dance
I move
I pause
Contemplating the importance
Of
the
moment
music awoke my spirit
the rhythm of him
resuscitated me
I am experiencing
jimi

Blues

Whatchu know about it
Cried about it
Cussed about it
Slammed doors and
Slid down to the floor
Trying to work that thang out
Pain on me like gout
But the only libation is liquor
And like trig with no calculator
I can't figure
Just missing X
And wondering Y
Not reading signs
Agony has me cosigning
But I don't want to take possession
Just stuck on this stupid lesson
Too many two cents
I don't want your change!
I crave my evolution
Conversation rebuking
When I only want to be held
Left to yell
What the HELL!

Whatchu know about it
You got solutions under your belt
Or just the urge to be engulfed in what I felt
Pulsating
Saturating
Deep in and deep out
Sighs and cries
And lies
A fist banging on doors
Slid down to the floor
Not a whore
But body leased
And the debt remains

And pains
Gain momentum
Wait
Contemplate position
So late in the game
But never too late
To change

Answer the call – Stand up or not at all
~ a response to the 911 calls

I cried for help
But you did not hear me
In hooded clothes you claim you fear me
In suits and ties you wanna be near me
In open spaces you joke and jeer me
Seems like I am the focus of your attention
Black and intelligent
Strong and dominant
No, we don't always get away
As you so calmly stated
Many of our freedoms are emaciated
Hundreds of thousands trapped behind the walls of a cell
Because no one heard them yell, and as a result they fell
Whether by choice or accident
That's still my brother – he is still missed

Where is Big Mama?
You think she would let someone tussle on her lawn?
She'd be turning the lights on and making some noise
Hollering, 'WHATCHU OUT THERE DOIN TO THAT BOY??"

Fear has us all cowering to the floor
Waiting for someone else to save who we adore
I am not sure what to say anymore
Since when did we become so weak?
What happened to the fighter in me?
Where the hell is the fighter in you?

Or are we so simple minded that, all we fight for are some shoes?
Fighting for a man that both women will loose
Sitting on Facebook pimping your little girl
And yourselves for that matter
Social media capturing ignorance and putting it on display
As your embarrassment floats across the world, what will you say

I'm frustrated with callowness

Keyboard gangsters trying to have cyber confrontation
Oxymoron
You fight for foolishness but not for a cause??
You can't fight in the street
'cause you too busy showing your draws!

It is an overdose of ignorance
And I am SICK of it
Wake up and feed your mind
Read, learn and expand your intellect
Until you burst with innovation
That will change this brain washed nation
Too many people suffer from diarrhea of the mouth
If you cannot elevate
Educate
Alleviate
Or edify

Shut up
There are enough idiots running amuck

Plateau

Why do we look at our mountain
As mountainous and unachievable
Mistaking fear for awe
You are not amazed
The beauty does not intrigue you
You are angry
Furious that this behemoth stands boldly
Scolding in soft whispers of you can't
Rope
Gear
Warrior paint
Libation so the spirit won't faint
I'm coming victory
I see you mountain top
This is one woman
You
Can't
Stop

Just Grow!

You so progressive
That you
Not
Progressing
You so aggressive
That you
Keep
digressing
stop serving liquid lips
dripping ideologies & pseudo biographies of what you wish
your life could be
but you too lazy to put the work in for

so upset that success takes work
you walking around being a jerk
In need of help
But you burned your bridges
A bleeding heart that can't get stiches
Coveting my riches
While you sit on your britches

Leave your pity party
and
start an evolution revolution
evolve from a state of being
To a state of doing
It is your future you need to be pursuing
Not the defamation of me
Cause
I'm
gone
Be
ALL
RIGHT!

Free

Taboo to you
Satisfaction to me
One, two or three
Don't frown
I let my guard down
& inhibitions
& limitations
Release to peace
Just free
But you not ready for that
From me
I'm a lady
With a lil hood in her
Don't ask how it got there; just is
Content minding my own biz
Checking
Recollecting
Socially free
Just because you're boxed in
Don't tread on me
I'm free dammit
No matter how uncomfortable that makes you feel

Resolution

But will the
Resolution come
Will the resolution come?
Raining down towers of confusion
And soaking the foundation of thought
Washing away seeds
God has not brought
Once cleansed and purged
Through and through
If tested will your heart be tried and true?

What will the resolution take?
Thoughts so powerful they induce earthquakes
Rationalization of analyzed nations
Getting your news from more than one station
In depth contemplation of your state of being
Or is it on your own mind that you intend on leaning
And the problem you chose not to resolve
Has turned on you and begun to evolve
And where is the conclusion
To your state of confusion
Or is it the truth that you are still refusing
Will you lie down and die over a little contusion
Where is the confidence
You're supposed to be using
And will this drama ever reach a final resolution
Or will you allow this disease to perpetuate itself
As you continue to strive for material wealth
Well you can't live peacefully off material possessions
Until you possess your soul
And so ends my message

Assata

I gotta laugh
You seem to think that
What you speak maps plans for me
Words secrete from your lips
But do not graze in my vicinity

You can't touch me

Oh you thought an older me would be
What?
Vulnerable?
I feast on wisdom daily
Meditate on Sun Zu
Tai chi at dawn
midnight rendezvous with Oshun

I'm Neo to your Mr. Smith
Jumping in your system
And flexing
My mere existence is vexing
But you ain't hexing
My roots flow through the swamps of N'awlins
vaporize through your residence
Inhale exhale
Circumvent
I prevail

Go on grit ya teeth
Form meetings where ignorance comes together to personify itself
My knowledge is wealth
But this ain't no bailout

You are entranced by my defiance
Enraged at the testimony of my life
You got strife?

Take it to the Lawd

I'm taking to my sword
Inking my legacy in gold
You knew I was bold when I took what was mine
Now I am courage multiplied
The mathematics of this equation you can't refute
Numbers don't lie
But you can't compute

"Science is organized knowledge. Wisdom is organized life."
Immanuel Kant

www.ingramcontent.com/pod-product-compliance
Lightning Source LLC
Chambersburg PA
CBHW020948090426
42736CB00010B/1326